Poems from the Sand

Carl R. Busby Sr.

authorHOUSE®

AuthorHouse™
1663 Liberty Drive, Suite 200
Bloomington, IN 47403
www.authorhouse.com
Phone: 1-800-839-8640

© 2007 Carl R. Busby Sr.. All rights reserved.

No part of this book may be reproduced, stored in a retrieval system, or transmitted by any means without the written permission of the author.

First published by AuthorHouse 12/3/2007

ISBN: 978-1-4343-5288-0 (sc)

Library of Congress Control Number: 2007909018

Printed in the United States of America
Bloomington, Indiana

This book is printed on acid-free paper.

www.poemsfromthesand.com
poemsfromthesand@yahoo.com

Dedication

This book is dedicated to the men and women of the United States of America Military, the Coalition Armed Forces and the Civilian men and women that support them in this Operation Iraqi Freedom effort. This effort in Iraq and Afghanistan has brought the support of common men and women from all over the world to come together as one to support the militaries in this fight. During this history making event, the everyday wife, husband, sons and daughters risk their lives daily to help make a better life for the local Foreign Nationals. Unfortunately in these efforts, there has been much blood shed in this quest to achieve victory. These brave men and women constantly face danger on a daily basis. As I go about my duties on a daily basis, I see many young people who have decided to put their lives on the back burner to support a mission that they believe in. Some of these kids are just out of high school, while the season veterans have chosen to re-enlist and offer their experience and leadership to the future of America. Then there is the group that many people don't hear about. This group is the men and women of the various contractors that have decided to help support the military effort. Many contractors have also perished in this struggle. It is this group that I am a part of. The majority of us believe that what we do on a daily basis is vital to the military effort. This is the first battle that civilians have gone to "Ground Zero" to support the military. Most people do not have a clue to what we also encounter daily until our next of kin gets a call that we won't be coming home the same way we left. It is this reason that I began to write and share my poems in hope of spreading joy, laughter and open the eyes of people all over the world to make them aware that "<u>we believe</u>".

Contents

A Mother's Love	1
A Fly Girl's Game	2
A Complicated Man	4
A Brand New Start	5
Another Christmas Holiday	6
Another Birthday Without You	7
A Real Lady	8
And You Say You Love ME	9
Be Still My Heart	10
But, It's a Girl's Backpack	11
Call Me Later	12
Classy Lady	13
Doing It Alone	14
Don't Deprive Me	15
Don't Drive Me Away	16
Don't Take It Lightly	17
Farewell My Love	18
Feeling Blue	20
Friends are Few	21
Get Your Act Together	22
Good Night My Love	23
Goodbye My Dear Husband	24
Goodbye My Sister	25
Grace Keeps Me	26
Happy Birthday Letter	27
He Came Tumbling Down	28
I Adore You	29
I Am A SOLDIER	30
I Bought It Myself	31
I Can't Take It Anymore	32
I Decided To Go To Iraq	33
I Had A Nightmare On Last Night	34
I Knew This Day Would Come	36
I Won't Be Coming Back	37
If I Never Called	38
I'll Go Next Sunday	39

I'm All Grown Up	40
It's Christmas Time	41
It Is What It IS	42
I'm On My Way Overseas	43
It's Time My Love	44
It Hurts The Same	45
I'm Not Perfect	46
I've Missed You	47
It's Her Game	48
It's Vegas Time	49
It's Your Face That I See	50
Just Because	51
Just For You	52
Kash Is Out	53
Lady "D"	54
My African Flight	55
My Bad	56
My Back Stabbing Coworkers	57
My Chapter Is Written	58
Momma, Why Do You Cry	59
My Love Is Genuine	61
My Dream Invitation	62
My Home Visit	63
My New Home	64
My Valentine	65
My Valentine, My Love	66
My Status Please	67
My Work Place	68
No Don't Mean NO	70
No One Cares	71
Not Meant To Be	72
On This Day I Promise	73
Only A Few	74
Right There With You	75
She Came My Way	76
Someone to Share - Someone that Cares	77
Standing Guard	78

Stop and Let Me OFF	79
The Big Payoff	80
The Brother – The Date	82
The Government Inspector	83
That Whistling Sound	84
The Lonely Nights	85
The Man Rules	86
The New Boss	87
The Midnight Run	88
The New Lady	89
The Night Walk	90
The Other Woman – Part (1)	91
The Other Woman – Part (2)	92
The Phone Call	93
The Power of a Woman	94
The World We Face	95
Thinking of You	96
To Have And To Hold	97
Tomorrow	98
Tripping On A Memory	99
What U Mean 2 Me	100
What's Really Going On?	102
When I Go	104
When We Met	106
Why Play Games	107
Yes I Do	108
Yes I Am THICK	109
Yesterday	110
You Are No LADY	111
You Came Into My Life.	112
You Will See The Light	113
Your Shield Came Down	114
Your Smile	115

Poems From The Sand…are the smiles, tears and happiness of the faces of many Military and Civilians who are serving in a far away country. These poems come from a voice and a heart of an inspirational soul.

About the author: <u>Carl "Reggie" Busby Sr.</u>

I met Carl in November of 2004, on a small camp name Ad Diwaniyah. Carl is genuine, not a pretender. He is kind, generous and helpful without any expectations. He is someone that you can trust, that you can call on to pick you up when you fall. He is a husband, father, brother, and a son, but most of all; "My friend". Carl has faced many obstacles in his personal life as well as on his job, but by the grace of God, he has accomplish his number one goal…writing his first book, "<u>Poems From The Sand</u>".

Take care and God Bless
Annie Fuller Dean
October 07'

POEMS FROM THE SAND... are a heart felt look into the everyday issues of the lives of Military and civilians alike here in the land of Iraq. This book of poems captures and echoes the true feelings of the heart. They are reflective of the various challenges and issues we all have to deal with being such a long distance from our homes. Thank you Carl for being the "voice" for so many lives in the land of the desert...

About the author: <u>Carl Reginald Busby Sr.</u>

I have known Carl since my first day at Camp Echo July of 2004. In a land that was truly foreign he took me under his wings. He is no ordinary man. He surpasses any man I have met. His heart is so genuine and caring. He has guided, and assisted me through some of my most challenging issues while being here in the desert. His heart is as huge as the universe. He has the ability to make things happen when others has given up on a solution. He is blessed beyond measure with the gift of writing. I am truly honored to be his best friend. It is so exciting to be a part of this chapter of your life. May God's "favor" and blessings richly increase in your life. Soar high my friend soar high. With God on your side nothing is impossible!

Mary L. White

"Poems From The Sand" is an extraordinary reading experience that one has yet to encounter. It speaks of the insightful and adventurous journey of living and working in the desert during the midst of the Operation Iraqi Freedom war and mission. The poems speak the truth of life, relationships, and marriages and the unknown things one could not possibly think of doing back at their own hometown. It displays the connection and disconnection between people ... the happiness, joys, promises, mysteries, lies ... and all that life encompasses.

About the author: Carl Busby

Insightful, creative mind, dedicated, and wonderful friend and co-worker whom I had the privilege to work with in Mosul, Iraq '07. His understanding of life's experiences and relationships is truly an art. His willingness to help a friend in need and go the "extra-mile" to get to know someone is amazing. Carl has truly been blessed with the gift of writing as a way of reaching out to others. It is a blessing to call him my dear friend.

~ Monica Reyna Sanchez ~
7 October 2007

About the Author:

Strength doesn't just come in the physical. It also comes in the strong at heart. With all the mothers, father, sisters and brothers that are giving of themselves and their families to work in The Operation Iraqi Freedom War and Mission for all of us. It has taken Carl many years to write these heartfelt poems. He has gone through and grown a lot over these past years. Being overseas is especially hard when you deal with losing love ones and the pain that it brings. But he has an extraordinary gift and ability to put into words what most all of us feel. Carl has been one of my closest friends for twenty years now. He has always been there with a kind word to lift my spirits, a good joke to make me laugh, or a beautiful poem to help me appreciate what life is really about. His loyalty to his family and friends alike is an outstanding quality. To have him as my friend has truly been a blessing to me. Thank you Carl for showing me throughout all these years what a True friend is like.

Stay Blessed.
Thea

A Mother's Love

A True Mother's love is very genuine,
It can't even be compared to the best of fine wine.
A true Mother will give you her very best,
It can stand up to the most stringent test.

When you have done all that you can do,
A true Mother will always stick by you.
You may think sometimes that she is rude,
She has to be because this world can be crude.

She started it all when she gave you life,
The hard times were on with all of your strife.
She was there to wipe your running nose,
Did you ever send her even one rose?

She dressed you and taught you many things,
There were even nights when she would sing.
Sometimes she had to do it all alone,
That was when the father figure was gone.

She didn't pout or put up a fight,
She knew that raising you took all of her might.
Some of you were blessed to have her a long time,
Still, there were times that you didn't send a dime.

A True Mother never really complained,
She knew in Heaven would she get her gain.

A Fly Girl's Game

Please don't touch and keep your hands to yourself,
As you can see, I'm here with somebody else.
I've got my part-time man with me tonight,
And everything is going just right.

This man is fine as all eyes can see,
Yeah, you're right he's here with me.
You see, my main man is overseas,
And sometimes I need my body pleased.

I got a call the other night,
And my man said he would be on an early flight.
He said that we would have the big talk,
I knew then that it was time for that aisle walk.

He came in on the early bird,
I think that it was on January 23rd.
I called my part-timer to buy me a fly dress,
I told him for your birthday, I want to look my best.

He asked would he see me on tonight,
I told him that Nature is here, the timing isn't right.
I went by and picked up a few bucks,
When I left, I had a quick chuck.

Don't judge me with that look of shame,
It's all a days' work in a Fly Girl's game.
I knew my man had to go back overseas,
This trip was made especially for me.

My man called and said, "Around eight, we'll do this thing",
I pondered and wandered, would it be the 4 or 5 carat ring.
I practiced for that right look of disbelief,
I figured I'll drop a few tears and sigh of relief.

He came through the door looking like a new Recruit,
All dressed in his starched stiff Marine green suit.
He started by saying, I heard of your part-time man,
He even had some pictures of us in his hand.

I wanted to talk and give my plea,
He said; don't try to run your tired game on me.
I was hurt he said, deep in my bones,
And then just like that, my main man was gone.

A Complicated Man

I'm a complicated man, some say,
I do a little of everything, then want it my way.
I'll bring the roses, dinner and wine,
I have no problem even going out to dine.

I'll spoil you in a minute and won't think twice,
I don't see a problem, it's just being nice.
You seem to think that it should be just you,
That's the big problem, because it's hard to do.

Most of our women have it hard each day,
The obstacles of life bring challenges their way.
The job, the bills and all of that you see,
They sometimes ask the question "What about Me"?

It's then I swing into action and show I care,
I treat them like a sweet teddy bear.
It's then that they want their very own,
The man, the car and the 4 bedroom home.

Some say something about "your cake and eat it too",
But the teasing and pleasing is refreshing to you.
Complicated may be stretching it, you see,
The problem is, there is a woman at home waiting for me.

A Brand New Start

I made a decision to give it my best,
I'm tired of always being the center of some mess.
I know that I haven't always worn my ring,
But it's time that I grow up and do the right thing.

You have been a dear and loving wife to me,
It's about time that I open my eyes and see.
I haven't always chosen to come straight your way,
And still with me did you decide to stay.

I played around almost all of my life,
And did everything to cause you much strife.
It is time for me to do what is right,
Or stop playing games and get out of your sight.

I want to hold you in my arms again,
Any other woman would only cause me to sin.
It wasn't easy for you to accept me back in your heart,
I really love you for giving me a brand new start.

Another Christmas Holiday

It was another disappointing day,
I waited and waited, but no personal call came my way.
I had an email that touched my heart,
It said that it was sad that we had to be apart.

If you are touched and feeling sad you see,
Then why didn't you make an attempt to call me.
Being gone can be a lonely thing,
It's not changed by the fact that you wear a wedding ring.

This year a few kids weren't so sad,
A call and the right gift made them feel all glad.
Even the big ones were able to enjoy the day,
Because good old Saint Nick also came their way.

It's not about gifts or even the reason,
It gets back to this joyous holiday season.
I will get through yet another day,
And realize that I'm angry that a call didn't come my way.

Another Birthday Without You

It's your birthday and again we are apart,
But no distance can keep you out of my heart.
I remember on the other night,
You said that my distance just didn't seem right.

I sent you a present, you see,
But you said that it couldn't replace me.
I know that I have been away rather long,
But I'm counting the days till I will be home.

I know and recall our many talks,
And the beautiful times that we shared on our walks.
But now I'm here and I'm doing time,
I didn't listen and I committed a crime.

I sit here and think about you,
Still wondering when I get out, what will I do?
I plan on working toward my GED,
So when I get out, I'll focus on getting a degree.

I do thank you for still believing,
Cause like many others you could be leaving.
It do pain me that I am away,
Especially on this being your very special day.

Happy Birthday

A Real Lady

I met a real lady, who seems so sweet,
She carries herself well and she is so neat.
You can tell by her actions she has been treated well,
Someone has shown her that life don't have to be hell.

She strides through the day with her shades on her face,
Her clothes are intact and everything is in the right place.
When she opens her mouth she has something to say,
She doesn't small talk but will wish you a good day.

She is a lady that exemplifies some real class,
Not like some of them that will turn as you pass.
She is short and petite and has it all going on,
Don't step out of place or she will let you know what's wrong.

She can light up any room just by stepping in,
Every now and then she laughs and has a very sweet grin.
A breath of fresh air is what she brings your way,
She can change your mood and brighten up your day.

A real lady is such a joy to see,
Everyone notices it and not just me.

And You Say You Love ME

You say that you love me without a doubt,
But your actions say you don't know what that love is all about.
I hear from you when you feel like making that call,
You say that you care but I don't feel it at all.

I've always been told that love is shown and not just said,
You don't know whether I'm alive or even dead.
When I called you there was laughter all around,
But your conversations keep saying that you are always down.

You tell me that you are going through a rough time,
But you say that you are a true friend of mine.
I tell myself that I'm being put to a test,
But I think that it is you that is not doing your best.

When I call to put you in your place,
You get all emotional and the tears run down your face.
You are smart enough to run me through your game,
But pretty soon my feeling won't be the same.

For now I'm going to sit back and wait,
Each day I stare at the phone and anticipate.
I'm getting stronger each day with no call,
I'm beginning to feel that you don't love me at all.

Be Still My Heart

My mind was filled with your beautiful face,
I embellished the thought of being in your grace.
Lately I've become overwhelmed with seeing you,
My daily routine is interrupted that I don't know what to do.

This is the first time that you have occupied so much of my mind.
Your walk, your talk, makes you are one of a kind.
I began to quiver and shook in my seat,
My heart started to race to a brand new beat.

I don't know what came over me,
Now I'm interested to find out what this could be.
I've talked to you many times in the past,
But never before did my heart receive a blast.

I wasn't affected until you told me your reaction,
Now my heart is beating fast and I may need traction.
It's been 10 minutes and everything is still the same,
It all started just by you calling my name.

I'm not a weak man and I'll give you my best,
If your lips ever touch mine, then that is the true test.
Your beauty and charm will make a lame man walk,
You can melt a pure man just with your talk.

I've always been a man that will do my part,
Just one word from you and you'll have my heart.

But, It's a Girl's Backpack

My momma made me carry this backpack to school,
Knowing that this girl's pack makes me not look cool.
I didn't want to carry this thang,
But my momma made me in all this rain.

My big brother started to tease,
My mother interceded and said, Johnny please.
I thought maybe an hour I could stay,
But the weather man said it would rain all day.

You need to keep your books dry,
I left out the door as she said goodbye.
My raincoat wasn't big enough to cover it,
I walked to school having a little fit.

I walked down the street feeling kind of blue,
When this woman called out and said, hey you.
I turned around just to see,
Who was this trying to address me?

She said that it was good that I was doing my own thang,
I said I'm only carrying this because of the rain.
She snickered and said, yes it is a messed up day,
I told her, maim, I'm not gay.

I told my mama how this day would be,
I was right; they are going to make fun of me.
I knew that it was going to be this way,
I just wish that I can make it through this day.

Call Me Later

I've been thinking about you from afar,
Just wishing I could be where you are.
I care for you very much,
At times it might not seem as such.

I've been under a lot of stress,
Going day by day without you is a test.
I may have acted a little weird late on last night,
But when you called, the timing just wasn't right.

I reached for my cell and it fell on the floor,
The noise you heard wasn't a knock on my door.
I was trying to find my phone in the night,
All the noise was me reaching for the light.

You know there is no one else that I want to see,
You are my baby and the only one for me.
The voices come through the thin walls,
They stay up all night and give no respect at all.

I'm very tired after a very hard day,
Can I call you later or send an email your way?
It's late in the night, somewhere around eleven,
You can do me a favor and hit me after seven.

Classy Lady

Look at the lady dressed all classy tonight,
Her game is smooth and her body is tight.
She walks around with an elegant stride,
Her steps are so graceful, she seems to glide.

As she walks my way, I get up from my seat,
This is truly one woman that I want to meet.
She looks me up from my feet to my head,
The dress that she is wearing was of a silky thread.

I'm Claudia as she did address me,
I made this voyage because you are a sight to see.
There are many men hanging out in this place,
Your charm and wit seems to glow in your face.

I beckoned to the bartender to bring us some rum,
I went in my pocket and offered her some chewing gum.
As the music began, her head started to move,
She closed her eyes and began to groove.

I couldn't help but stare at her face,
Even her movement was all full of grace.
She stood up and reached for my hand,
I slowly got up and we started to dance.

We danced to the music all night on the floor,
She whispered in my ear and we headed for the door.

Doing It Alone

You are a good person and could be a good friend,
But you have a nitch for making the other person bend.
You had to grow up fast and quickly become grown,
You've worn the pants way too long.

A lady you are and a lady you seem to be,
Whether you choose to stop wearing the pants will be something to see.
It's a hard thing to do when you have done it your whole life,
You thought that it would become easier when you became a wife.

As the children began to grow and you did it alone,
It became apparent that you couldn't let your guard down.
You gave him every opportunity to be a man,
Soon you realized that you had to resort to the old plan.

You pondered and pondered on just what to do,
You realized that you had to do what's best for your children and you.
I've taken all I can take and I can't take no more,
I'm putting back on my pants and sending him out the door.

I'll do it alone and that is my plan,
A new opportunity awaits me in the Holy Land.

Don't Deprive Me

Why do you always make me wait?
Knowing that being with you is all that I anticipate.
You come around me with that beautiful smile on your face,
Walking all nice and with so much grace.

I'm doing my best to treat you with charm,
What I really want is to hold you in my arms.
I've got patience and I'm doing my best,
Girl you are continuing putting me to the test.

I don't know how long I can continue to resist,
The months that you were gone, you were really missed.
I continue to sit back and do my part,
My every waking moment is on the woman that has my heart.

Your words are few and your voice is so sweet,
The first time you blessed my eyes, I knew we had to meet.
I'm going to continue to sit back and admire from afar,
Dreaming of that special day when I'll be where you are.

Don't Drive Me Away

It's rumored that we don't stick around,
But the truth is that you are always putting us down.
Some are deserving of the treatment that they get,
Still there are others that won't even think about it.

You say that we don't know how to treat you,
But you curse us out until your face turns blue.
You bust us down whenever you can,
Then you say that I am not a real man.

Whatever happened to a gentle hug and a kiss?
It's those little things that I sorely miss.
I go to work and deal with mess all day,
When I get home, sure I'm anxious for a little play.

You sit home all day and now you have a little pouch,
That's the result of watching reruns of Oprah and sitting on the couch.
I'm going to sit for a while and get off of my feet,
You ask when I am going to get something to eat.

Did you cook at all or even attempt to bake,
You turn toward me and give me the Black woman's shake.
The head, hands and fingers began to flare,
Those are the times that I wish I wasn't there.

I hang in and pray each and every day,
That I don't succumb and be driven away.

Don't Take It Lightly

We go about working in this big open range,
Knowing that any minute, things could change.
Some days are quiet and without any stress,
Things sometimes get hairy and it becomes a big mess.

The rainy days are cold and make things all wet,
It's nothing like you've seen, this I will bet.
Some summer days are as high as 150 degree,
When the winds are gusty, you can hardly see.

To go on the roads it becomes a high risk,
There are treacherous things out there that can change it to bliss.
We get on a bird and fly through the sky,
Even that's not so safe; you have to keep a watchful eye.

Convoys have become a thing of the past,
Every now and then; they are hit with a blast.
They won't come out and fight like a man,
They hide around and plant stuff in the sand.

We haven't began to rebuild Iraq,
We have lost many soldiers that can't come back.

Farewell My Love

Well, it's been almost a year,
Since the last time that I held you near.
I've been counting down the days,
Cause being without you is like living in a maze.

I found it hard to sleep last night,
Just knowing that in two days I'll meet your flight.
I laid down and tried to close my eyes,
In anticipation of a quick sunrise.

I dozed off and started to dream,
Or at least that is what it seemed.
I came to the airport with a flower in my hand,
I could hardly wait for your plane to land.

The plane landed right on time,
And I knew that you would soon be mine.
You exited the plane with tears in your eyes,
So I figured it was from all the joy inside.

I saw your daughter and son at the airport too,
I guess they were all there to meet you.
You greeted each of them with a kiss,
I knew that they were also missed.

I was at the back of the crowd you see,
So it was hard for you to see me.
I shouted your name until I was almost numb,
But for some reason, my way you did not come.

You guys seemed to be in a rush,
And when I missed you, my little heart was crushed.
I darted to my car to get there quick,
My stomach was beginning to feel very sick.

When you got in the car, you were dressed kinda cute,
But for some reason, you changed into a three piece suit.
You got to the mortuary and went right in,
I figured you stopped to say goodbye to a friend.

I had my black suit on, so I went right in,
You were sitting down waiting for the service to begin.
I moved quietly toward the front so I could see,
And to my surprise, it was ME.

Feeling Blue

I didn't sleep well on last night,
My guts were tossing like everything wasn't right.
You see I got some disturbing and troubling news,
That I couldn't share, not even with you.

My lady started a new email romance,
It seems to be a pattern of her taking a chance.
I really want to believe that it's just another friend,
But with all the secrecy, this may be the end.

I want to have this special lady in my new life,
But I can't stand to deal with another uncaring wife.
I'm trying to stay calm and not tip my hand,
It's hard to do thinking she has another man.

I want to bring it up and put it on the table,
But my fear is that this relationship won't be stable.
I really love this woman you see,
But I'm developing doubts if this is my wife to be.

If I don't get sick trying to hold it all inside,
I will see how long she will let this ride.
So right now my world seems gloomy and turning gray,
I guess that is the first sign that it's not going to be a good day.

Friends are Few

Sometimes when we don't know what to do,
We search for our friends, but they are few.
We build relationships of many kinds,
But we discover that it's only in our mind.

When I'm troubled and I need to talk,
I find it helps if I take a long walk.
The walking helps to relieve my mind,
But it only last a very short time.

I pick up the cell to make a call,
And there is no answer, no answer at all.
I left a message on the voicemail,
But your response is slow as a snail.

You always seem to brag and boast,
Where are you when I need you the most?
I've got to get me some better friends,
Some that will be there through thick and thin.

I don't want to lay on you this guilt trip,
But I find it better to shoot straight from the hip.
I don't need any money, not even a dime,
All I need is just a little of your time.

When you can spare a moment or two,
Let me receive a call from you.
I know that you may have to make a tough choice,
But sometimes, I would just like to hear your voice.

Get Your Act Together

You say that you love me without skipping a beat,
Is it really love or you just swift on your feet.
The words that you say, do they come from your heart,
Are you another brother who is just playing a part?

You say that your words are the real thing,
Do you plan on following them up with a wedding ring?
You come over about twice a week,
Is that love or comfort you seek?

We have been at this for better than a year,
I'm living a nightmare is my worst fear.
I got in this relationship for the long haul,
Your actions show that you have been having a ball.

At first you said that you had to get a job,
Instead you decided to steal and rob.
I moved in and you decided to go straight,
Lately you have been coming in very late.

I'm getting tired of your same old game,
The results are generally always the same.
I'll give you a week to get your act together,
Or you will be singing a new tune in some very cold weather.

Good Night My Love

I made my bed, now I must be a man,
I never wanted to insult you; I only wanted your hand.
You are a one and only kind,
All I ever wanted was for you to be mine.

I never ever thought of you as something cheap,
To do that would make me one of the filthiest creeps.
Don't accuse me of being like that,
I do consider myself a little bigger than a rat.

I'm guilty of trying to show off my greatest find,
But I must move carefully if I want her to be mine.
You see I never knew what true love could be,
Until you came into the life of someone like me.

I'll work on getting things right in my life,
Cause I do want you to be my wife.
If for some reason you shall want another,
I only hope that he will be a worthy brother.

For me, I'll continue to go down and pray,
In hope that we will still have our day.
I never wanted to go to sleep,
Ever feeling this much like a creep.

But as midnight began to fall,
I could not get a call through, not even at all.

Goodbye My Dear Husband

I'm going home on the next available flight,
If I'm lucky, I'll get there tomorrow night.
It seems there's a crisis at home you see,
The legal system is calling on me.

I came here to help change my life,
But instead, I'm going home to divorce my wife.
I've checked the account or what use to be,
And it seems my wife has all but drained me.

I've been working here all this time,
What you've done to me should be a crime.
I trusted you and called you honey,
Then you go and clean out all my money.

I called and talked to a few of my friends,
They each said that it sounds like it's the end.
I tried not to get very irate,
But there's only so much that I can take.

I should be there soon if you want to talk,
She said no thanks; I'm getting ready to walk.
I'm leaving your clothes, truck, and you can have the cat,
Oh, by the way, I'm taking the baseball bat.

I'm through shedding the nightly tears,
And I've gotten over my early fears.
So goodbye and have a good life,
So long from your former wife.

Goodbye My Sister

I talked to my sister just the other night,
It was something about her voice that wasn't quite right.
She was happy to hear from her little brother,
She always told me that I was like none other.

I always loved to hear the cheer in her voice,
Her words were true and not just rambling noise.
She would ask when are you coming this way.
She said you have been gone many a day.

What is it like way over there?
Some days it's good, others not so fair.
Is there a danger being in that land?
I would say my life is in God's hand.

I tried not to talk about things in Iraq,
Most people don't even know where this country is at.
When are you coming back home to stay,
My anniversary date is the 5th of May.

One Sunday morning when I got out of bed,
I received a Red Cross message that my sister was dead.

Grace Keeps Me

I arrived on this Army base in May,
I will never forget that hot summer day.
There were hardly any clouds on the scene,
We were open to the radiant sun's beam.

It gets pretty hot in this desert sand,
The temperature gets as high as 155* in this land.
My relatives wondered if I were in a bind,
Most of them thought that I was losing my mind.

I was supposed to be the smart one you see,
This action wasn't what was expected of me.
They hugged me and shed a tear or two,
My eldest niece said "Uncle I love you".

It didn't bother me as I planned to depart,
I knew that there was one on high guiding my heart.
I listened a lot to my gospel songs,
Some days I wondered if my decision was wrong.

God has kept his hand on my head,
If it wasn't for him, I surely would be dead.
I do my part to run this challenging race,
As I know I'm protected by his mighty grace.

Happy Birthday Letter

I'm writing you this letter today,
Because there is something that I want to say.
It's your birthday, this I know,
I can tell because your face is a glow.

You dressed for the occasion as I can see,
Unfortunately, it's for you and not for me.
You are working those clothes of black,
I don't know who ever told you, but that's where it's at.

You look like you just got off your thorn,
Girl, you deserve to be in that brand new home.
You walk so right with every stride,
Displaying all of your true feelings inside.

I keep telling myself don't venture down that lane,
So I'm holding back the feeling and dealing with that thang.
I really know what I must do,
And that is to avoid a situation with you.

You can bring a strong man to his knees,
You can do it with the way you like to tease.
I looked at you and wanted to flip,
I did all I could to stop from kissing your lips.

I'm trying to restrain and stay out of your way,
Especially on this being your birthday.

He Came Tumbling Down

My friend decided to call it a day,
It was around 3 years that he did stay.
He began to work out to tone down his belly,
We all knew it had something to do with a girl named Kelly.

This guy knew how to entertain his friends,
He would invite women over to shake their rear ends.
You see, he had this tall pipe called a stripper pole,
They came from miles around to dance with this stick in the hole.

The women were amazed and wanted to see this thing,
They didn't even entertain the thought of a ring.
Sometimes it was easier with a drink or two,
When you added a little music, they just knew what to do.

They all wanted to take their turn,
The room was smoky as the cigarettes burned.
The men would loudly chant, go, go, go,
Pretty soon all the clothes were on the floor.

My friend made up his mind that the timing is right,
He said that it had nothing to do with what happened the other night.
He went to a wedding about a month ago,
It was he and Kelly that walked through the door.

Now he is struck by Cupid's love bug,
I give him 6 months before he's walking down the rug.
He will soon have to give up the smoking and skoal,
And pretty soon, up will come the stripper pole.

I Adore You

There has always been something special about you,
It's not found in all women but just a few.
You possess all of the qualities of a pure breed,
You have everything that a good man really need.

The stride of the peacock is in your walk,
Words of wisdom are displayed in the way you talk.
There is nothing more beautiful than your charm,
You are definitely a woman that is above the norm.

The things that you do, just because,
Makes most think and grown men pause.
You don't go around bragging like it's all about you,
You bring the sunshine out and turn the grey sky blue.

I always knew that you had a heart of gold,
You make a strong man weak and a gambler fold.
You can hold your place besides any man,
To keep up with you is a challenge if he can.

My heart goes out to you in every way,
You know just how to make my day.
Just talking to you gives me a new start,
You will always have a special place right here in my heart.

I Am A SOLDIER

I sat down to talk to the soldier man,
I am truly amazed in his life in this sand.
I have a true passion for the things you chose to do,
That is one of the reasons I chose to help you.

The soldiers and his friends talk about the plan,
To bring some peace and love to this Iraq land.
They were told that it wouldn't take as long,
But now they realize that the politicians were all wrong.

We were given the speech of how we liberated Kuwait,
But this Iraq land seems to present a no ending date.
We hear gossip and rumors about this very rich soil,
But we hope that we are not here fighting for this oil.

I've lost a few friends in this treacherous fight,
Unaware of the obstacles that they faced during the night.
We share a common bond and back each other,
Regardless of the creed or color, we are all blood brothers.

Sometimes I wonder if what we are doing is right,
Then I remember the bodies from the insurgent plight.
They don't want any peace in this land you see,
They have no guilt about killing themselves or me.

So we adorn the uniform, the helmet and vest,
Then we proceed out the gate to our next great test.
We go down on our knees with our heads bowed and say,
Lord help us make it through just one more day.

I Bought It Myself

I finally got a new Home for me,
I bought it myself as you can see.
No, it was no man that paid the price,
Although it would have been really nice.

I worked long hours for this new house,
And yes that means I am the boss.
The furniture, the appliances, I did it all,
I bought everything enclosed within these walls.

If you plan on visiting me at this site,
Call me in advance and give me a few nights.
I don't mind a visit from my friends,
If you don't call first, then it might be your end.

I like my place and I value my time,
If I invite you for a visit, bring a bottle of wine.
Don't come looking for a bite to eat,
Especially if you didn't buy any meat.

I'm going to sit back and look ahead,
And relax in my big king size bed.

I Can't Take It Anymore

I can't continue to take your crap,
You spoiled my day and woke me up from my nap.
My sleep is very important you see,
It's one of the things that I do just for me.

You come in the door and raise your voice,
It's nothing more annoying that all of that noise.
You complain about the food and you want it now,
When I cook, you tell me I don't know how.

You can always go back home to your mommy's place,
You're no help to me in this rat race.
Your mommy can cook and she apparently knows how,
You can look at your sister being big as a cow.

I brought you in and gave you a place to lay your head,
You sleep all day in my king size bed.
I thought that you said you had a decent job,
I didn't know it consisted of trying to steal and rob.

You check the mailbox each and every day,
I didn't know you had a check coming this way.
You ask me when will we get paid,
If you mess with my tax check you will feel this blade.

I'm giving you until the end of the week,
So you have 5 days of looking for a job to seek.
At the end of the week we will sit down and talk,
If things are the same, your bags and you will walk.

I Decided To Go To Iraq

I decided to go to Iraq one day,
I was on the manifest for the 5th of May.
I left somewhat under a confused cloud,
Mainly I didn't know what to expect at all.

I saw the news and all of the bloodshed you see,
I had doubts about that happening to me.
I was approached and told they had something new,
But I had to keep it quite; there was only room for a few.

I went to find out what was at stake,
That's when they told me that I was going to Kuwait.
The news was exciting for me to hear,
I don't drink, but I was willing to have a beer.

After many hours I arrived at my new workplace,
It turned out to be a big military base.
Everybody there seemed to carry a gun,
At the first loud noise or boom, I was ready to run.

On the 4th day another meeting was called,
This time the news wasn't good, not good at all.
We are all moving, so go get packed.
We are going up north to the land of Iraq.

Some was confused and said it wasn't right,
They fought it and complained with all of their might.
I thought real hard about this being a bad deal,
But I realized that I came here to pay my bills.

We had a choice to return to Houston town,
But 9000 miles was too far to come and turn around.
I was among the few to head to the new land,
Now my new home was to be in the Desert sand.

I Had A Nightmare On Last Night

The dream started with me listening to some rap,
I lay across the bed and decided to take a quick nap.
When I woke up it was very late,
I called and said I'm sorry about our date.

I will have more time on tomorrow,
Not realizing it was your time that I was looking to borrow.
I overslept and realized that you hadn't come back my way,
I looked at the clock and noticed that it was yet another day.

I noticed that it soon turned to night,
And I thought that it couldn't be right.
I picked up the phone and placed a call,
And to my surprise, there was no answer at all.

I jumped in my car to take a ride,
In anticipation of being by your side.
I went to your window and threw a small rock,
Because I wasn't sure if it was alright to knock.

I went to the door, because it was the right thing to do,
I realized it was the only way that I would see you.
There was no answer to my knock you see,
I then wondered how this could be.

I returned home and there was this letter,
It was from you, and I felt a little better.
It said, Dear Baby I stopped by your place,
But I missed you on my way to the base.

I got a call that said I was re-activated you see,
So you missed the opportunity to see me.
I'm sorry, so I'm leaving you this note,
Cause I have to hurry and catch the boat.

You will never know what I was bringing your way,
All because you was gone on that day.
But because you didn't savor our time,
I'm leaving you with this single dime.

I'm off to the deep blue sea,
Unfortunately, that was the last time that you could see me.
I woke up and realized that this couldn't be,
Cause you are the only woman that's right for me.

Then I said this I can not bare,
And then it struck me, it was only a Nightmare.

I Knew This Day Would Come

I've searched and searched for the right words to say,
I always knew that you would be leaving someday.
Although we never got the chance to explore each other,
You probably thought of me as just another brother.

I've always known that you did exist,
But I stayed my distance and tried to resist.
I really enjoy a woman with grace,
Then it's easy when you have a beautiful face.

Your body is well maintained and all so right,
You can even make a blind man see the light.
It's a little late to think about the past,
Now that your time is approaching really fast.

Some things are better kept away from the crowd,
I'm a man with a big heart and I don't talk loud.
It has been great knowing a woman like you,
Now that you are leaving, I'm feeling kind of blue.

I hope you the best in your next stop,
You have everything to offer and you will never flop.
I bid you farewell and continue to be yourself,
You will always carry in your heart the place you just left.

I Won't Be Coming Back

It was very hard to sleep last night,
One of my friends had gone to fight.
I know he was just doing his job,
But it seems like his childhood was robbed.

He went out wearing the USA flag and feeling proud,
During the night the blasts were very loud.
This was all real and it wasn't a game,
But the families are looking for someone to blame.

It's hard when you are many miles away,
You constantly pray for them to have a safe day.
The time is closing; it's been almost a year,
You ask for the Lord to remove all of your fear.

You glance at the TV to see what is new,
The commentator says in Iraq we lost a few.
It was something about what was said,
It didn't go away; it stayed in your head.

You lie in the bed and try to get a nap,
It's then at the door do you hear a tap.
Who is it this morning on this June Day?
It's too early for anyone to come my way.

I look and noticed the Military men,
I invited them in and we sat in the den.
Before they could begin to talk,
I went out the door and took a short walk.

I got the news about some things in Iraq,
It amounted to my son won't be coming back.

If I Never Called

If I never called, would it bother you at all?
It is that feeling that makes me climb the wall.
I write and write, with nothing ever said,
I can understand because you never read my mail.

I use to get a card every now and then,
The last time I got one, I don't even know when.
What could this mean that you don't say?
Could it mean you are getting tired of things going this way?

Words without action is pretty lame you see,
It's worse than not saying any word to me.
I still wait and wonder if you will call,
At the end of the day, there was still nothing at all.

I'm trying to regroup and wipe my eyes,
Then I realize that it is a final goodbye.
I won't wait by the phone anymore,
I finally got the guts to shut the door.

I'll Go Next Sunday

I go to work each and every day,
I work so hard there's not much time to play.
It's hard doing it alone, but I know that I can,
I'm thinking about getting me a part time man.

I really don't need a man every day,
Just until I can began to see some daylight my way.
Monday and Tuesday I'm running around,
Wednesday is hump day and it's time to get down.

Thursday and Friday were kind of rough,
It's the weekend now and I'm ready to strut my stuff.
Saturday is here and I could hardly wait,
I'm just undecided about who will be my date.

It's Saturday night and the bar closes around two,
I'm a little tipsy and dancing, I don't know what to do.
I better sit a while because I almost had a fall,
Could someone stop the spinning of the wall?

Well, it's Sunday morning and I can't make it for church,
Lord you know I need my rest, tomorrow is work.
I'll make it next Sunday, this I'll promise you,
Today I'm all tired, what is a girl to do?

I'm All Grown Up

When I think about how the time has gone,
I often think of you, the one whom I belong.
We have shared many good times together,
Through the good, bad and even the stormy weather.

I have not always been the very best,
There were many times my patience was put to the test.
You have always stood firm in your belief,
You offered me comfort and shelter when I needed relief.

When I was wrong you had to set me straight,
Those were the many times that I didn't appreciate.
I have grown up and I'm out of the house,
Someday in the future I'll get my own spouse.

I've found that this world can be really cold,
Those things that glitter may just be fools gold.
I'm living my life and running in this race,
I'm doing everything I can, not to catch a case.

I'm all grown and I'll call you when I can,
Right now I'm upset and calling you is not in my plan.
Just give me my space and don't bother calling me,
I'm all grown up and doing my own thing as you can plainly see.

It's Christmas Time

The lights were flashing on almost every house,
No cars were moving, not even a mouse.
The snow was falling from high in the sky,
The kids were hoping that St. Nick would stop by.

For the fortunate kids, each family had two,
For the single mom, it's a struggle just to make do.
Some will inherit a big credit line,
That's the thing to do, to buy on time.

Even though we struggle to make ends meet,
Just to hear our kids say, wow that's neat.
I'm trying to work a few extra hours,
To stay afloat and have a little more green power.

This day has brought many families a rift,
Because they have forgotten the real true gift.
It's not about the new things that were bought,
It's about the Love that he truly brought.

It Is What It IS

We received a new boss to our group,
For once he wasn't military or part of a troop.
He came in waving a big stick,
Someone told him that he had to be strict.

He is a former athlete and he played the game,
Nothing came of it and he wasn't a household name.
He journeyed up north and landed in Mosul Iraq,
At least there he didn't have to wear armor on his back.

He found the new site to be a much quieter land,
But all wasn't as easy as he had planned.
This group had just gone through a big ordeal
There were personnel heads rolling like a tumbling wheel.

New people had rolled in from various places,
Everywhere you looked, there were new faces.
I was one of those that was also new,
My old bosses were skipping out too.

It worked for the best as Mr. D displaced our fears,
His famous statement every morning is "it is what it is".

I'm On My Way Overseas

I joined the military because it just seemed right,
I had no ideal that I would be going to fight.
The recruiter told me that we're not in war time,
Now that I look back, he should be charged with a crime.

I was told of all the benefits and the house I could buy,
All of this is true and good if I don't die.
I signed all of these papers and my life away,
When I told my parents they didn't know what to say.

My mother started to cry and could only say WHAT?
My daddy said that I wasn't too big for him to still kick my butt.
It didn't matter that I was an only kid,
They just couldn't believe what I had gone and did.

I started to workout and get my body in shape,
Pretty soon the call would come and I'll have to adorn the cape.
Now that I have more time and I began to look back,
I realize that the day is coming that I'll be going to Iraq.

I signed up to protect our USA land,
Now the fight has moved to the desert sand.
I'm heading across the waters to the desert soil,
I hope I didn't enlist to fight for OIL.

It's Time My Love

You came to me on last night,
It was after you had been in another fight.
You know you have to leave this man,
You said you are going to as soon as you can.

I held you close to my heart,
Knowing that it pains me when we are apart.
I told you, in my arms you belong,
But you tell me that it seems so wrong.

I tell you that it's no love in that place,
And he will send you to an early grave.
You say that I just don't understand,
But I told you that he can't be much of a man.

You know that I will treat you kind,
But this you will have to accept in your mind.
You made up your mind to be free,
And now you are just waiting on me.

It Hurts The Same

I was hoping that this day would never come,
It was news that made my body feel so numb.
The news was that my old camp grounds had been hit,
The impact was so bad that it made some people quit.

We had been hit many times before,
When you hear that sound you normally hit the floor.
This particular rocket had a mission,
The news would sink some family into submission.

The rocket had a destructive plight,
It hit the laundry as it began the night.
Although I didn't know this particular one,
It hurts the same when another life is done.

She had only been here for a short while,
But now her family would have to bid a farewell goodbye.
We all chose to work in this dangerous place,
But I couldn't stop the tears from rolling down my face.

This camp in Iraq was my first home when I went abroad,
It's been three years and I'm still on the Iraq sod.
Lately there has been death all around,
I do my best to keep my feelings from staying down.

We send up prayers to the higher power above,
We are kept each day by his everlasting love.

I'm Not Perfect

I'm not perfect as you can see,
Because I realize that I can only be me.
I have misjudged a friend or two,
I didn't realize that I made a few kinda blue.

I acted a little shallow a few times too,
Please don't take it as a direct reflection on you.
I value the times that you woke up to talk,
You could have easily told me to take a walk.

I do care and love you with all of my heart,
I'm not just saying that because we are apart.
I value true friendship as a treasure,
Being around you is always a pleasure.

Most times I try to do the right thing,
But there is sometimes I don't act like a human-being.
I promise to never forget who have always been there,
And I will always remember to be fair.

If I get complacent and don't share my time,
Just remind me that I still consider you a friend of mine.

I've Missed You

You have been gone for quite a long time,
I often picked up the phone and thought about dropping a dime.
Then I thought about the times when I did call,
I didn't receive a return, no return call at all.

It use to feel so good just to talk to you,
You knew what to say to bring me out of the blue.
I remember the times when I came your way,
You always made sure that we enjoyed the day.

It's been about 4 months and I haven't heard from you,
I was so confused that I didn't know what to do.
I know people get busy and lose track of the time,
But you have always claimed to be a friend of mine.

I've sent a letter and left a message on your cell,
Who knows, you might be somewhere off in a jail.
I would hope that it is not the case,
By the lack of communications I might not be far off base.

From my distant seat in this far away land,
I'll sit back and come up with an alternative plan.

It's Her Game

It's her nature and claim to fame,
They are the ones that invented the game.
The rules are made and changed at their will,
Pretty soon they will move in for the kill.

They will work on you right from the start,
It won't take long before they have your heart.
We try hard and give it our best,
But we have no tools to withstand their test.

We may stand fast and win a few rounds,
That is when we get knocked to the ground.
A woman is a gift from the man above,
She comes our way with the art of love.

We have the right to just say no,
That is when we get put out the door.
Some believe that we can put up a good fight,
Then some know that we don't have the might.

Some of us consider our self to be a pimp,
Those are the ones that fall like a wimp.
It doesn't matter whether we are young or old.
We soon realize that it's better to do what we are told.

It's Vegas Time

I traveled to the city full of lights,
It's known for the glamour and Vegas fights.
The hotels are a beautiful sight to see,
The life itself is what entertains me.

I'm destined to go to a few Vegas shows,
The women are beautiful and their headband glows.
They danced all around on the stage,
The main acts were lowered down in a cage.

The band played some of the most fantastic songs,
In this city where nothing is considered wrong.
I drove up and down the Vegas strip,
Then I cashed in a bill for some poker chips.

I played blackjack and hoped for twenty-one,
After spending all of my funds, I was soon done.
The days seemed to go by really fast,
I went home broke but I had a blast.

It's Your Face That I See

It's your face that I'm seeing every night,
My illusions of you just don't seem right.
I wake up each morning somewhere around two,
I can't continue like this but I don't know what to do.

Your face has such a beautiful glow,
I'm hoping for the day that your show me to your door.
You carry yourself in such a ladylike way,
It's getting hard just trying to have a normal day.

Now again I'm seeing your graceful face,
I'm having thoughts of being in your place.
It has to be rough when you are a lady with charm,
There is always some man wanting to be in your arms.

Sometimes I sit back and think of what you will do,
If I suddenly expressed the feelings that I'm having for you.
It can't be real because I've known you for only a short time,
But true affection is altered when it comes to the mind.

I'll continue to admire you from afar,
While I suppress my desire to be where you are.
I'm going to try to go back to sleep,
As I fight the feeling and desire to creep.

I will have to work on staying in my place,
While I lay back down and vision the smile on your face.

Just Because

I was thinking of you all night long,
No it wasn't anything you said that was wrong.
When I got up I sent some flowers your way,
It was just because this is another day.

I've taken them for granted, the friends that I know,
Lately I've been running and staying on the go.
It's time that I take a moment and reflect,
On the things I have and the people I respect.

I don't have many people that I call my friend,
At least the ones that will be there through thick and thin.
Most of the things that I do don't have a cause,
I do it without reluctance, no cause at all.

I may send an arrangement or just a single rose,
That may depend on how my love for you grows.
Needless of the fact that it doesn't take a reason,
Something good will happen regardless of the season.

It may not happen today but sometime down the line,
You will get some flowers along with a bottle of fine wine.

Just For You

I thought that I would send a gift or two,
To show my true feelings I have just for you.
I'm not trying to introduce a ring,
I'm still enthused by the romance thing.

We have known each other for a long time,
There were even times that I thought you were mine.
A woman of many parties, you used to be,
That wasn't very attractive to a man like me.

I sat back and watched you change your ways,
I considered making a comment on many of days.
A year went by, then two and three,
I wanted to make sure that you were indeed free.

You changed, developed and were no longer down,
That was the true sign that you were becoming all grown.
I like the new woman that you have come to be,
Again I say that you are the woman for me.

Kash Is Out

It was the last night that Kash was on the scene,
She was heading to a new Iraq home to do her own thing.
Everyone was there on this beautiful night,
They came from all over to see Kash out right.

She held her own and maintained her place,
She was one of a kind and a lady with grace.
We were saying so long to another beauty,
She was a beautiful woman and a great cutie.

Kash is a woman that spoke her mind,
If you were slow on the draw, she would leave you behind.
She maintained her cool during summer or fall,
She smoked her brown cigar around the t-wall.

I thought that she was too cute for the cigar she smoked,
But she was so cool, not once did she choke.
Kash chose to go to a brand new place,
She would be successful with her beautiful face.

At least she left under her own clout,
The last thing she said is "Kash is out".

Lady "D"

Lady "D" was her given nickname,
Beauty and charm was her claim to fame.
She could walk in a room and men would stare,
If I was with her, it was like I wasn't there.

The looks and the body, she has it all,
She is 5 feet 5 and not too small.
Her skin is smooth and fair to the bone,
Her hair is natural and of a dark tone.

She has a voice that makes me melt,
It's hard to explain just how I felt.
I never saw her get extremely mad,
Not even once despite the conversations that we had.

She has no wants from any man,
She makes it on her own, yes she can.
I'm delighted that she calls me her friend,
She'll stick by your side through thick and thin.

This beautiful woman is great to see,
The nickname I gave her is Lady-D.

My African Flight

It was time to branch out to see,
What would the continent of Africa have in store for me.
I never really wanted to go to that land,
It was the farthest thought from my plan.

While over here in the Middle East,
What would be the harm in seeing a few wilder beasts?
I boarded the plane with Kenya Airways,
At the start of this trip I was truly amazed.

To my surprise the pilots and crew eyes were not blue or green,
But all of the airplane staff was like me – you know what I mean?
It made me feel warm and all good inside,
To see this new team that was coordinating the ride.

I buckled down in my seat for 6 hours to stay,
I lowered my head and begun to pray.
No, it wasn't because of the airplane staff,
I really don't enjoy flying on any aircraft.

The flight was normal and there's nothing more to say,
The crew greeted us and said have a nice day.

My Bad

I gave you a call the other day,
To tell you that I was coming your way.
Again I was told that you were not in,
Because you were hanging out with your new friends.

How is it that you say it will get better,
But you are out there trying to be a player.
You pop in – right out the blue,
It's been three days since I last seen you.

You come in feeling all mighty,
Then want me to put on your favorite nightie.
You wreak all over from the smell of beer,
Then you say, why don't you come over here.

I sit back and say that we need to talk,
Then you look at your watch and get ready to walk.
I go in my purse and pull out a dime,
I tell you to call when you have some time.

You get up and walk out the door,
I don't know what kind of fool you took me for.
I made a pledge that night you see,
You won't be lying in my bed with me.

I thought about it all that night,
And I wondered if I was being right.
As I drove to your house, I said you would change,
A second car in the driveway seemed kind of strange.

I used my key that you gave to me,
Because the driver of that car, I wanted to see.
I opened the door all mad and bitter,
To my surprise, I was dealing with a switch-hitter.

My Back Stabbing Coworkers

I educated myself to be all that I can,
I had hopes of someday reaching the management land.
It took blood, sweat, and sometimes tears,
I was destined to overcome all of the fears.

Stage one and two were the learning phase,
I kept striving and reaching for my destined place.
I dressed each day the professional way,
I wanted nothing to spoil my triumphant day.

After many years of doing my job,
My day was coming and I wouldn't be robbed.
It was my big day that finally came,
I had reached the group in the managers' game.

I continued to spin off my brilliant ideals,
My coworkers began to plot and show their fears.
It didn't matter whether they were white or black,
It was all about making me fall flat on my back.

Lies and deceit was in making,
It was my butt that was there for the taking.
Trusting my brother wasn't a hard thing to do,
Because you knew he had your back when it came to you.

It wasn't the case as I did see,
It was my ethnic brother that had it in for me.

My Chapter Is Written

Maybe it is customary that you must cry,
But let it be known that isn't the way to say bye.
I lived a good life while I was alive,
I worked hard and tried to strive.

Some people will miss me and that's alright,
But practice restraint with all of your might.
I was a descent and caring man,
I did my best in the race I ran.

Some will say that they are tears of rejoice,
Others will boo-ho just to make some noise.
Some came to me when they had something on their mind,
Others left with the notion that I wasn't very kind.

I couldn't help everyone but I did my best,
There were many times that I was put to the test.
I traveled to many places near and abroad,
I even spent some years on foreign soil.

The time has come that I can now rest my feet,
My life is done and my maker I'm waiting to meet.
So to my family, friends, my son and wife,
My chapter is now written in the book of life.

Momma, Why Do You Cry

Momma, I've been thinking about the words that you said,
From my younger years as I lay on this bed.
You always told me to make up my own mind,
To treat others right and always be kind.

I remember when you taught me to ride my bike,
You even took me fishing and on my first hike.
It was never a big deal that my childhood was without my dad,
You comforted me when he passed while I was a young lad.

Most of the time, I didn't think much of school,
I was preoccupied with trying to be cool.
I use to think that school was for the nerds,
Hanging out with my friends, that was the word.

I hung in there and realized it a little late,
That caused me to graduate at a later date.
You told me to hang in regardless of my age,
On that May date you were proud when I walked across the stage,

There were many times when I sneaked out of the house,
Those were the days when I challenged you as being the boss.
You cautioned me about doing that, which was right,
I didn't want to hear it so I simply dropped out of sight.

I still didn't do right and spent a little time in jail,
All because I thought it was cool to steal someone else mail.
I did my time and learned a good lesson,
I thought to join the military would be a blessing.

I carried a weapon and I thought that I was bad,
I still didn't understand why you were so sad.
Now I am laying here because of a roadside blast,
All I can do is reflect on my very illicit past.

I can't move my body but I can still hear,
Other relatives are around you and saying I'm sorry mommy dear.
I feel pretty good and seem to be complete,
I was shocked to hear you say "cover him with the sheet".

Now I know why it was that you cried,
It's all because someone said that he had died.

My Love Is Genuine

The Love that I have is Genuine,
It's only dispersed some of the time.
I give my Love clear and free,
You see that's just the guy in me.

I don't give my love just to appease,
If you believe that, you really don't know me.
Sometimes I think that I want too much,
I never believed that things could be as such.

It's not the big things that you do at all,
It's just the opposite, the ones that are small.
I try to imagine that everything is the same,
But to believe that I wouldn't be true to my name.

Sometimes just saying my name was a joy,
You handled me like a million dollar toy.
I know that my feelings are true,
Sometimes thinking this way makes me feel blue.

I must raise my head and look toward the sky,
I'm still praying and believing in that man on high.
I will keep my peace and don't say a thing,
I still want to do that which involves the 5-carat ring.

My Dream Invitation

I got my call for the Oprah Winfrey Show,
What to expect, I just didn't know.
I wasn't one to tune in each and every day,
I had planned to get my TV antennae sometime in May.

To some people it's almost like a junkie's crave,
They will be watching it when they go to their grave.
I tuned in when it was very new,
It's not many that lasted, only a few.

The show has the ability to make or break,
That is the chance that many are willing to take.
She tells the good and exposes the bad,
Some people go there trying to look sad.

I don't have an agenda or a claim,
I'm not even trying to get any fame.
I've written something that is important to me,
If it goes somewhere, I'll just have to see.

As I sit here waiting for my turn,
This is something that you will have to earn.
I'm sitting all alone with no one here at all,
I know pretty soon I will get my call.

I've waited a long time for this day,
It's the result of the many times I did pray.
I'm sending my shouts to the Good Man above,
He blessed me again with a show of his love.

My Home Visit

I've been gone for quite some time,
I'm ready to head to that home of mine.
The years are becoming very long,
The United States is where I belong.

I came up here to do my part,
Or at least to get a new financial start.
The beginning started off kinda rough,
There were many times that I had to stay tough.

Many lonely nights have passed me by,
I had to man-up so as not to cry.
I have seen many come and go,
Some didn't last a month before hitting the door.

I thought about going home a time or two,
But I realized that I still had a mission to do.
I would call and talk to a few friends,
They all wanted to know when this war would end.

I'm not making any of the rules you see,
I can't even control what happens to me.
I put my life in the man on high,
And each day he helps me get by.

I'm going home pretty soon,
I should arrive there a little after noon.
I'll spend my few weeks on the USA land,
Then I'll have to return to the Desert sand.

My New Home

I've got a new home that is being built on high,
Some has said that it's somewhere in the sky.
I'm not sure what kind it will be,
I will just have to wait and in time I will see.

Some days there is grief and stress,
I try not to be consumed by all of the mess.
I stay the course and try to be brave,
Some folks would drive you to an early grave.

I go about trying to do my best,
Every way I turn seems to present a test.
I sometimes struggle and even fall,
It doesn't bother me, not even at all.

When I fall I land on my knee,
That is the place that I really want to be.
While I'm there I raise my head to pray,
And that is the way that I end my day.

So my home is being built anew,
I hope you are preparing because there are only a few.
I don't know when I'm going to that place,
Where it's not about the swift, but who finish the race.

My Valentine

To my Valentine I present my heart,
This is the beginning of a brand new start.
I've known you now for a little more than a year,
And still you still bring me joy and cheer.

I wanted to make this a very special day,
Then I realized; it has been special since you've come my way.
When I first noticed your beautiful smile,
I was so overwhelmed I was willing to walk a mile.

There were times when I would drive and come your way,
I didn't have a clue to what I was going to say.
I knew that I had to just see your face,
So I just drove or even walked to your work place.

Some days I was feeling all sad and blue,
It was then that I had to see you.
Sometimes I would open the door and just take a peek,
Then my attitude and mind-frame was shaped for the week.

I remember when I was shot with the arrow of Cupid,
I was so baffled that I thought I was going to say something stupid.
I decided to shape my life and do my part,
With hopes that you will continue to occupy a chunk of my heart.

I want to thank you for giving me a chance,
To experience the gift of true romance.
So with my heart, my soul, my mind, I wish to say,
Thank you for making this a Great Valentine Day.

Happy Valentine Day

My Valentine, My Love

My Valentine you are so dear to me,
My love is still strong clear across the sea.
I miss you already; it's only been a day,
I'm tempted to catch a plane and head back your way.

My nights are sleepless and seem very long,
The passion of your love keeps me holding strong.
I walk around sometimes with my head in the sky,
My heart filled with remembrance helps me get by.

I often reflect on when I left out the door,
I realized I had a job that I was leaving town for.
It wasn't as bad when you was my bride to be,
But now you've become my wife and the woman for me.

You walked down the aisle and took my hand,
On that day in town, I became a proud man.
The honeymoon was full of excitement and joy,
You would have thought I was a man with a million dollar toy.

The fireworks was on and my voice was high,
Everyone would have thought it was the 4th of July.
We returned and began to build our home,
My time was short and I knew I had to roam.

I departed my love and the USA land,
But I carry you in my heart into the desert sand.

Happy Valentine Day

My Status Please

I called you late on yesterday,
I had a few words that I wanted to say.
We have been seeing each other for more that a few years,
Heaven knows that dealing with you has caused me many tears.

I realize that you are single and free,
But that is why I want to know what you think of me.
Certain days and nights, you choose not to answer your phone,
This brings me to wonder what is really going on.

You told me that your feelings for me run deep,
But each night there is no call before I go to sleep.
I can reach you early in the morning hour,
But your disposition is very sour.

It is coming down to us having a walk,
That seems like the only way that we can have a talk.
It's not that I don't have feelings for you,
But you leave me wondering what to do.

Now you can give me my unconditional release,
Or just tell me what my status is please.

My Work Place

I sit here and work all day,
Accepting the little money that you call my pay.
I know that I can do better,
That's why I'm considering my termination letter.

I can do much better than this,
Coming here every other day, feeling all bliss.
I've been working here for almost 365 days,
And you keep telling me that I must change my ways.

I'm getting ready for my yearly review,
I'm going to see what you are going to do.
You say that merits will be based on facts,
Again I feel that this whole thing is just an act.

You wanted to schedule it on a Monday you see,
But you know Mondays are not good for me.
Tuesday or Wednesday will be a better take,
Yeah, I believe that either will be a good day.

I came to work on Thursday this week,
I wore my best suit as I was looking rather sleek.
My review was scheduled for right after lunch,
I got there at 2pm, right after the crunch.

I sat there and waited, it seemed like all day,
Then 15 minutes later, you came my way.
We went over my folder and my face got red,
I could have stayed at home in my bed.

I thought about my party scheduled for that night,
Contemplating my raise that I felt was right.
You just shook your head as I continued to talk,
You made a call and then took a walk.

Finally the door opened and Security came in,
Followed by the Personnel officer with a company pen.
I was wondering how much my raise would be,
The Personnel officer said read on and you will see.

As I read on I was truly amazed,
I thought about setting this whole company a blaze.
I got my raise to the next floor,
Then Security escorted me right out the door.

No Don't Mean NO

Apparently, I learned something new today,
I learned that No doesn't mean what it say.
I asked a young girl what no mean to you,
It meant holding her breath until her face turned blue.

I finally decided to conduct a test,
And come to a conclusion which answer is the best.
One person said no is only a means,
To get what I want-it might have to be a scene.

Another said that no means we are apart,
Then it's time to negotiate and bring in the heart.
Sweet J said no means I have some negotiations to do,
Just give me a little while and I'll have him feeling blue.

Still another said I'll tell you the way it is,
It means getting a yes might involve the pill.
Taking a pill and what will that do?
It might involve me getting x-rated with you.

So no don't quite mean what I originally thought,
Which was everything on that matter had come to a halt.

No One Cares

Another Holiday has passed me by,
And no one called, not even to say Hi.
I sat by the phone all day long,
Just wondering what was really going on.

I didn't expect a flood of calls,
But what's with that, not one at all.
I came to work on the next day,
Still there was nothing that came by way.

I will try to forget and let it go,
This steam is building inside and I'm ready to blow.
I must get it together and not be down,
Put a smile on my face and remove the frown.

As I regroup and try to remain calm,
It's hard to forget as my arm is getting numb.
I'm going to get up and go for a walk,
I really don't want to hear anyone talk.

I'm supposed to have at least a friend or two,
They should come through when I'm feeling blue.
I know I don't have much of a life,
I understand no call from my uncaring wife.

It's ok, I will get through all of this,
Flatten out my hand and unclench my fist.
I guess this is the test of "through thick and thin",
I'll bring it to a closure and let it all end.

Not Meant To Be

We decided to take a road trip together,
Being it summer or winter, we didn't mind the weather.
We will be together doing our own thing,
Some people might call it a romantic fling.

I packed my suitcase and headed out,
I couldn't believe all of the things that she brought.
I asked are all of those suitcases just for you,
You know I am a girl so what am I to do.

I decided to chill and get on the plane,
Now the nasty weather came and it began to rain.
The plane ride was about 6 hours long,
When I awakened I had a crook in by neck from sleeping wrong.

I asked for a double-vodka to get me through the trip,
She complained about that, I thought she had flipped.
We landed and went to a upscale hotel,
She mentioned the room had somewhat of a smell.

I was all ready in bed as she finished her shower,
She told me to get up, I smelled kind of sour.
I was told to pick my drawers up off the floor,
She was ready for dinner and pranced out the door.

She complained about things not being just right,
I knew I was in for a hell of a night.

On This Day I Promise

On this day, I give you my hand,
I promise to be your one and only man.
I'm giving up the entire women clan,
I keep saying, oh yes, oh yes I can.

I have no reason to keep up the game,
So don't even think of placing the blame.
I've found the right woman for me you see,
And I plan on making her my wife to be.

In the past I chose to have a few,
But that was mainly because I hadn't met you.
I searched all over, high and low,
And behold, she was right here at my front door.

I kept my eye on her for a long while,
To be sure that she was the one to walk down that aisle.
I have to go and tell others the news,
To some it's no big deal, to others it's the blues.

It came down to making up my mind,
Whether I wanted the 10 or settle for the nine.
I narrowed the field down to just a few,
I narrowed it a little more, and it was just two.

When I looked at the one, there was a little concern,
Whether later in my life, would I eventually get burned?
The other one was nice and sweet as can be,
But sometimes she showed she wasn't about to put up with me.

Now I wasn't GQ or even six foot two,
But I know that every day, I would please you.
So now I'm sitting, thinking and wondering which way,
I'll know something definitely when I go home in May.

Only A Few

When the world seems cold and your friends are few,
This is when I bow my head and began to talk to you.
Lord I have not done all that I can,
No, I have not followed your beloved son plan.

I go to sleep sometimes without going on my knees,
But as soon as I have a pain, I say "help me Lord, please".
Sometimes I don't always follow my heart,
But that is my fault, because your son did his part.

I don't read the Bible as I should each day,
I know that it holds the truth, the light and the way.
I sometimes walk through some days in a daze,
It's like my life is being lived in a maze.

During these days when people are dying all around me,
I should be getting myself together and closer to Thee.
From this day forward, I'm making a new plea,
To be more obedient and stay on my knee.

Our father which is in the Heavens above,
I thank you for giving your everlasting Love.
To this day I pledge my life anew,
It's so sad that it's still only a few.

Amen

Right There With You

I was thinking of what could I do,
To make it seem like I was right there with you.
I even thought of trying to jump on a flight,
But the time span would encompass about 4 nights.

That's the biggest problem about being in this place,
It lacks all of the beauty of a familiar face.
I go to sleep early each and every day,
Thinking of when I will be coming your way.

In the beginning my doubts was up in the air,
Getting through some days was like fighting with a bear.
The traveling consist of staying on my feet,
At the end of each day, I was constantly beat.

During the summer the weather is very hot,
Being in this place was like a melting pot.
I thought that I had paid the ultimate fee,
Then I saw it all when the weather reached 150 degree.

I work long hours, but the pay is good,
I would stay in America if I economically could.
But I have made bills above my head,
My financial picture use to stay in the red.

I signed on to stay for just a year,
When I did I was full of fear.
Working here is not always that bad,
Except when I remember the things I had.

I find myself still working beyond my year,
I think that going back to America is the true fear.
I'll continue to stay and work each and every day,
Don't worry, I'll soon come back home to stay.

She Came My Way

When I saw the woman with the beautiful eyes,
I scaled her body and noticed her shapely thighs.
She was a beautiful sight as all eyes could see,
I lost my train of thought as she looked straight at me.

I thought that maybe this would be my day,
She began to walk and came straight my way.
I didn't want to stare and act like a fool,
So I stood my ground and tried to be cool.

She came my way and asked if she could sit,
I thought any moment now my heart would quit.
Before she could speak or even talk,
I was mesmerized by the way she walked.

I stayed calmed and collected my thoughts,
I still didn't know what this was all about.
I could not believe that this woman was conversing with me,
As we sat there smiling for all eyes to see.

I guessed that finally it was my lucky day,
When this gorgeous woman spotted me and came my way.
We talked and laughed well into the late hour,
She gave me her number and left under her own power.

Someone to Share - Someone that Cares

I talked to my friend on the other night,
She said my timing was oh so right.
She was in pain and needed to talk,
It's during those times that I go for a walk.

I know all about the pain that runs deep,
Sometimes I get by myself and began to weep.
I decided to end and get out of this thing,
Twenty years ago it came with a 5-carat ring.

I'm deserving of more respect to come my way,
Not just on an anniversary or a special holiday.
Many years of devotion to just one man,
Not many women would, not many women can.

Sometimes you have to do what you know is right,
It normally means bearing it with all of your might.
I've got to stand tall and not be down,
Put a smile on my face and wipe off the frown.

I'm a strong woman with a good heart,
The time has come when we must depart.
I wish you well with the rest of your life,
Make her your partner, your friend and not just your wife.

This is something that I have to bare,
When I get weak, I know I have friends who care.

Standing Guard

The soldier is standing guard all through the night,
They stay up there to make sure everything is alright.
It's a dangerous job to take that stand,
They are guarding our lives from the militia-man.

The insurgents are there planning a way to get in,
The things that they do should be considered a sin.
It's nothing for them to use a little kid,
Their tactics are something that we would forbid.

When nighttime arrives and we all go to sleep,
The soldiers stand steadfast to make sure the bad guys don't creep.
We wake up early at the dawn of day,
Unaware of anything that might have come our way.

We say that each of us has to do a part,
But the enlisted joined because it was in their heart.
These brave men and women come from all across the land,
They all met up in this desert sand.

I do what I can to have peace in my heart,
At least I believe that it is a start.
There is nothing that can replace a life or limb,
Especially from those making a decision based on a whim.

I go on my knees nightly for the entire group,
I pray that HE protects our military troops.

Stop and Let Me OFF

I don't like what this world is doing to me,
I'm getting stressed as all of you can plainly see.
I go to work for many hours each day,
And I still can't seem to find my way.

I call home to hear a cheerful voice,
Instead all I get is a lot of noise.
I hang up and call a friend or two,
Each of them seems to be feeling all blue.

I turn to my computer to get out of this rut,
Each game I play, the computer kicks my butt.
I head for the door to go for a short walk,
Then there is my freaking boss saying we need to talk.

I can't win for loosing as some people might say,
I know that this just isn't going to be a good day.
My life seems to be going in such a twirl,
Just stop and let me off this messed up world.

The Big Payoff

Hello to my new found friend,
This is the guy you met, nicknamed Gentle Ben.
I'm sending you this short telegram,
To let you know just where I am.

I had to leave rather quick,
Because I wanted to be here to get first pick.
You see I received this important letter,
That said my life was about to be all better.

The letter said that I had inherited a lot of cash,
So get here early for the big bash.
It said that My Uncle Sam had recently died,
I didn't even know him, but still I cried.

I got there early and proceeded right in,
I never realized that I had so many kin.
I had on my new 3-piece blue suit,
It went real good with my new suede boots.

The letter said I had a lot of money coming you see,
I understand that my Uncle Sam had been looking for me.
The room was full as the man began to speak,
I wished that he hurried, I had plans to keep.

Ok, Ok, let's gets everyone signed in,
Don't use pencil, but use the black ball point pen.
Shut the door so that we all can hear,
I'm sure each of you plan to celebrate with a cold beer.

The money was on the tables for all eyes to see,
I still didn't know how much was coming to me.
With all that money, Security was very high,
They were all in the back, and on all sides.

Finally the man started to speak,
I'll be quick because you probably have plans to keep.
He said that he was Captain Leroy Trust,
And that we all need to raise our hands, this is a Bust.

There were ATF, Police, FBI and the FEDS,
There were even some with plain clothes and dreads.
Some of us stood and wanted to run,
But we were afraid, because they all had guns.

He said you are all on one of the lists,
And he thanked us for coming and we were no longer a risk.

The Brother – The Date

You hide your feelings as only you can do,
Whether it's good, bad or just feeling blue.
You say that you have had a rough time with men,
Most of the ones that I've dated should be locked up in the pin.

I met one the other day that had a thing about being the boss,
But I couldn't get over the fact that he lived in his mother's house.
How can you feel that you can run things?
The fake Rolex, gold teeth, and cheap bling, bling.

I was impressed with the restaurant as we sat down,
You told me it was the first one you saw that was downtown.
When they brought the menu; you began to drop,
You took out your billfold and said "how much do I got".

He looked at me and said "we might have to economize",
I spoke back to him and said "we should have just super-sized".
He looked again and said; oh I got my card,
I thought to myself at least that is a good start.

We ate, we talked and the mood was just right,
He asked if he could come over and stay the night.
I was feeling good and I thought, what the heck,
He read my face as the summoned for the check.

I got up to go and refresh my face,
When I got back he had a look of disgrace.
Amazed and unbelief ran through my mind,
This brother's card had just been declined.

I went in my purse and gave the waiter my card,
Then I looked at my date really, really hard.
I'll pay you back at the end of the month,
I said don't worry, you've just been dumped.

The Government Inspector

The Government compliance woman is again on the prowl,
She doesn't take any mess, no excuses at all.
She will go about doing that what she must,
Don't get caught messing up or another will bite the dust.

When she comes your way, have your timesheet right,
Or you might end up having a very rough night.
She will listen to what it is that you want to say,
Then she will leave and go about doing business her own way.

Don't think about bending the rules even one time,
You might find out that she will drop you like a hot dime.
You may think that she has a grudge against you,
But that's all about what a government officer do.

There are many rules here in this sand,
Some of them will get you sent back to your homeland.
One rule says that you can't drink alcohol,
Not even one drink, not one at all.

So when you see the government rep stepping your way,
You can rest assure that it won't be your day.

That Whistling Sound

It was almost dinner time on that day,
When all hell seemed to come our way.
It started with a loud whistling sound,
If you heard it before, you knew something was wrong.

I've heard that sound many times before,
A few moments later I was heading out the door.
It's a sound that begins to affect your mind,
The result of what it does is not very kind.

Whether you are at work or laying it down,
It makes a loud noise when it hits the ground.
The week had been somewhat quiet,
But today, those missiles seem to have a guide.

The 1st one came in and hit the empty land,
But the 2nd one found our property can.
By the grace of God they all made it out,
As the last person made it to safety, there was a big shout.

Everyone headed for the security of the shelter,
This was the start of a true helter skelter.
They came in one after the other,
When you thought it was over, then there was another.

The final count on that day was around ten,
Some thought this day would be their end.
There were men and women, black and white,
We all pitched in and helped on that night.

I prayed to the Lord as I kneeled to the ground,
Again he saved me from that whistling sound.

The Lonely Nights

The nights up here seem very long,
When you finish 12 hours you become withdrawn.
Each day consist of a long 12 hours,
By the end of the day you have very little power.

Many come here not knowing what to think,
The atmosphere could change, quick as the eyes can blink.
Some days it is like being at home,
All that is missing is the fact you can't roam.

You are enclosed within high T-Walls,
They surround the camp and are at least 15 feet tall.
You get to eat three free meals each day,
Some even get their own private place to stay.

After work some people have a 2nd life,
I've even heard that some have a desert wife.
I'm more into watching the TV,
A satellite, DVD, and a $2 movie.

Some days it can get very loud,
At times I've even seen a mushroom cloud.
During the night, you can't sleep too deep,
If you turn in early, you can get about 6 hours of sleep.

The Man Rules

Early each day during the break of the morning hour,
You can hear the repeating words coming from the large tower.
It is words and prayers coming from afar,
But you can hear them regardless of where you are.

I have always wondered what he say,
But no one is normally around so early in the day.
It is always done by a man,
Not many women speak publicly in the desert sand.

Some women are standing to take a bigger stand,
But their chances are bleak in this Arabic land.
Even the young males have a larger role,
And the women are generally left out in the cold.

Our Western women are use to speaking their mind,
But here in this land, that might not be too kind.
This is the land of the free swinging men,
Any other gender, they consider a sin.

Keeping your head low and knowing when to speak,
Might keep the average woman around for at least another week.

The New Boss

My new boss came in with a clear opened mind,
He had no ideal of what he would find.
The department was influenced with all types of diversity,
Pretty soon he discovered it was full of adversity.

He stated that we would all work as a team,
Some people thought that he was having a bad dream.
He is a bold man standing about 6 foot three,
His athletic build makes him as firm as a tree.

In his former job, he had a weekly meeting or two,
With his new job he has so many he doesn't know what to do.
He comes in early and stays real late,
Sometimes he rarely has time for a descent plate.

He stands firm and holds his ground,
He understands that some want him to fall down.
It's tough being at the top,
With people all around pushing for a vein to pop.

The top can be a lonely place,
Especially when you have to overcome your race.
Not all people was happy to see him come in,
But they hold their tongue and put on that stupid grin.

Sometimes he has to exemplify tough love,
Because someone is trying to see what he is made of.
He is a survivor and everything will turn out alright,
He don't have to worry, I'll help him through this fight.

The Midnight Run

They headed out somewhere around late night,
It was normally the time that they prepared to fight.
The night vision goggles were in their hand,
It was time for battle on this Iraq land.

Some of them weren't very old,
But still it was about doing what they were told.
They enlisted not knowing the full scoop,
They just weren't prepared to wear the combat boots.

Some had a gun that was as big as them,
Their uniforms were sewn with a 4-inch hem.
The helmet was made to withstand some lead,
But some of them were going to their death bed.

It was bitter and the night air did bite,
That was another obstacle as they prepared to fight.
Before they left they did kneel and pray,
I was hoping that they all would just stay.

I looked toward the heavens and asked God why,
Then I lowered my head and said goodbye.
They left the camp to fight on this distant land,
Some say it is all in the Almighty plan.

It was off they went on this Iraq sod,
I hope that they all made their peace with God.

The New Lady

I spotted you the other day,
When you smiled and looked my way.
I noticed your eyes you see,
Caused they were looking straight at me.

The next day I came to the same spot,
Hoping to see the lady that was looking very hot.
You showed up running kind of late,
But when I saw you, it was worth the wait.

I approached you this time and said,
My greetings to the fine lady dressed in red.
I invited you to have dinner and wine,
And you thanked me and said, "That's fine".

We ate and began to talk,
Then we agreed to take a walk.
We walked together along the shore,
It was all so good, seemed like I've done it before.

We both agreed that it was getting rather late,
So we discussed continuing on another date.
I wanted to meet on the next night,
But she said the timing just wasn't right.

A little disappointed, I said ok,
You said don't worry, it will be another day.
I asked for the number of your cell phone,
You told me that you had no minutes and it wasn't on.

I felt sad and began to feel blue,
You made me a promise that a call would come from you.
As we walked, I thought we had walked rather far,
I was wondering when would we reach her car.

I pondered and wondered what would become of us,
That's when you surprised me and said here is my bus.
My shocked face began to turn blue,
I couldn't do anything but bid goodbye to you.

The Night Walk

As soon as it turns dark and most people are asleep,
That's the time when the night crawlers began to creep.
They move in and around the various T-walls,
Their intention is really not to be seen at all.

The nights are dark and there is very little light,
But to a creeper, the time is just right.
It's not just men but women creep too,
Most creep because it gives them something to do.

Some have crept for so very long,
They have no respect and see nothing as wrong.
It's not about being black or even white,
What's done in the dark will come to the light.

Some creepers will tell you to maintain your part,
Don't get all wrapped up and let it involve the heart.
Then there are those that say everything is so right,
They just want the chance to spend the night.

Whether you creep quietly or let it be known,
Don't get pissed when your cover is blown.
Men and women will gossip and talk,
Especially when it's not them doing the night walk.

The Other Woman – Part (1)

I met my dream man at a club one night,
He was built so fine and looking all right.
From his head to his toe, I admired everything,
It didn't even bother me that he wore a wedding ring.

My eyes met his and I knew that it was on,
He looked like a king sitting on his throne.
I'll give him his props for being all cool,
I don't want to approach him and act like a fool.

He sat back and stared with those big brown eyes,
I wasn't about to lose this one without a proper goodbye.
I walked over to him and extended my hand,
He stood up next to me and I had to use my fan.

The music that played was all nice and slow,
He held me all close as we danced on the floor.
His warm breath on my neck made me firm and straight,
I knew on this night, I'll be going home late.

We left around 10 and I knew this was a start,
Right now I'll be the other woman and that is my part.
Being the other woman is not a bad spot to be,
There is the wife at home and then there is me.

The Other Woman – Part (2)

Being the other woman don't have to be all bad,
But the things that happened this week made me sick and mad.
I made an appointment to meet my man's wife,
Her job was one that enabled her to use a sharp knife.

I waited in the empty room for her to come,
I rehearsed this all night so that I wouldn't seem dumb.
She walked in the room and I noticed her big ring,
I thought about how she was married to my king.

After 3 minutes of talking, my phone went off,
I told her I'll reschedule; this is just a simple cough.
My goal was to look and get to recognize her face,
I had to get up and go before I up and catch a case.

Now this is the thing that tripped me out that day,
I saw my man and another woman heading down the freeway.
I buzzed his cell phone and there was no answer you see,
I pulled up besides him so that he could clearly see me.

I buzzed him again and he picked the cell up,
I don't want to complain or interrupt.
Are you with the wife and he said yes,
I knew then that I was in a big mess.

I got off the freeway and went right to his home,
His car kept going as he decided to roam.
I broke down to his wife and said he has violated your trust,
I can't believe your husband is cheating on the both of us.

The Phone Call

I received a call the other day,
It came from the states, rather far away.
I said my name followed by hello,
When I heard the voice, I nearly hit the floor.

I had only heard this voice a few times,
But it was one that sticks in your mind.
She said hello, do you know who this is,
I said sure, this is Liz.

I just got in from a long flight,
But I have a few questions if you have time tonight.
I'm thinking about applying for Iraq,
Because I hear that is where the cash is at.

Is it a long and gruesome process?
And is it a lot of work and a hard test?
I saw on the news where it gets very hot,
Is it like that all over, or just in certain spots.

What is the work like that I can do?
Is there any opening where I can work with you?
I'm ready and preparing for the 12-hour days,
Do I have to work a whole year for my 1st raise?

I'm planning and I'm ready for Iraq I'll come,
I'll be ok, until I hear the first bomb.

The Power of a Woman

Women have power, so I have been told,
Some are vane, deceptive and very bold.
They will smile and tell you to come their way,
When you get there, they say it hasn't been a good day.

They ask you to massage and rub their feet,
Then an hour later they send you for something to eat.
You drive all over town just to make things right,
When you try to stay over, they say no, not tonight.

Call me tomorrow and I'll be feeling better,
Then all of a sudden, you get a Dear John letter.
You open it with anticipation of delight,
Only to find out that she left town on an early flight.

You scratch your head and ask can this be true?
You don't want to believe that she is making a fool of you.
I've got a lot riding on the line,
I can't give up because she is too fine.

There must be something that I can do,
She can't just leave me out of the blue.
I have my pride but I want my woman back,
Maybe I'll buy her a black Cadillac.

I'm going to sit home and wait for her call,
I'm trying not to bang my head against the wall.
When she gets back, I won't cause a scene,
I might just get her another diamond ring.

She called me and said that she had spent all of her money,
So I went the store and sent a wire to my honey.
I'll call you when I get home,
Until then, I want you to wait by the phone.

The World We Face

I'm walking along a long dark street,
I feel no one else is around, only me.
My world is collapsing and closing fast,
I keep having the remembrance of somebody's past.

This world can be a cruel and awful place,
You can see it in the looks on most people face.
I use to think that I was one of a kind,
It's not me at all that is losing my mind.

The young folks are still trying to find their way,
The seasoned group is hoping just for one more day.
People are shooting classmates in the school,
It seems like everyone is acting like some kind of fool.

Our soldiers are dispatched all over the world,
Just seeing them die makes me want to hurl.
Most of our men are locked up in the pin,
When is all of the mess going to end?

Jobs are downsizing and letting people go,
Education is high and money is low.
Diseases are rampant and spreading so fast,
It seems there is no stop to the price of gas.

Where is the love that once was here?
When we met on the corner and shared a beer.
This is a world where there will be no peace,
Until we hear the big boom, then all things will cease.

Thinking of You

As I sit here in reminiscence of the past,
I'm smiling from head to toe, because we were the cast.
We have had many good times as I can recall,
But then, any time with you could not be bad at all.

We laugh, play and have fun with each other,
The only thing that can compare would be to have a twin brother.
I sometimes wonder if it's all a dream you see,
Because I never knew that all this happiness could be on me.

It's during these times that I'm feeling kinda blue,
Cause I'm a million miles away from you.
What I would give up today,
Just for a chance to come your way.

It's no picnic being over here,
Especially when I can't have you near.
I'll continue each day to watch the clock,
And dream about the times we walked around the block.

I'll sit here content writing this letter,
In hopes that soon, times will be better.

To Have And To Hold

I met the beautiful woman of my dreams,
At least she had everything to me it seems.
She had the looks and the body that gave me a thrill,
This girl was the one that would be a test of my will.

At first sight I knew she was the one,
Now it was up to me to just get it done.
I had practiced many times for this day,
Now I've lost my speech and I don't know what to say.

I stared at this gorgeous creature dressed in all blue,
I pinched myself and wondered could this be true.
Our eyes met and we talked without a sound,
No more with any other woman would I go round and round.

We began to talk and she was very cautious along the way,
I didn't want her to think that I was just another man on the prey.
We became good friends and that lasted quite a while,
We knew we were destined to walk down that aisle.

For a few years we stayed committed and became a pair,
In this day and age that's considered to be very rare.
Finally we decided to make a scene,
And let everyone know that we would be doing the wedding thing.

We knew that obstacles could arise and things could get cold,
But we vowed on that day to have and to hold.

Tomorrow

I'll do it later is what I said,
Right now I have a lot going on in my head.
You came to me just out of the blue,
Then I'm wondering what you want me to do.

I can't stop just because you showed up,
Personally, I think it was rude for you to interrupt.
But I am nice and I'll listen to your complaint,
I'll stay composed and practice restraint.

You said that it concerns some personal things,
It sounds like you should talk to the one that has the other ring.
Still I'm here and I'll open up my ear,
It's only right since you are my peer.

Now you want to get away and go for a walk,
I guess it's probably time for us to talk.
I'll be ready some time this afternoon,
Don't rush me because it can't be anytime soon.

It's around five and I'm making the call,
When I got to your office, you weren't there at all.
To my dismay I thought this was a horror,
I left a note that I'll see you tomorrow.

Tripping On A Memory

It's another night and I'm out with my crew,
When I'm with them, I'm not thinking about you.
I'm not saying that you are out of my mind,
But tonight I don't have to listen to you whine.

I'll be in when the club closes down,
But we are celebrating a birthday out on the town.
I do remember that I have a spouse at home,
It's Friday night and I'm going to roam.

Don't wait up I'm going to get in pretty late,
You remember what it was like when we use to date.
I'm not driving so I may have a drink or two,
To get in the right mood it may take a few.

I changed my clothes because I was looking a little lame,
Back in the day I was considered to have game.
The music was loud and I still had my groove,
I was out on the floor doing some fantastic moves.

The time went fast as it approached the hour of three,
I looked at my watch and realized I must flee.
Don't worry about it, your crew has your back,
I got up and realized that I didn't want to pack.

I got to the door and the bedroom light was on,
I hoped that I wouldn't regret the day I was born.
I got in the shower without a peep,
I was hoping that I could just go to sleep.

It wasn't what I remembered it to be,
But those were the days when I used to be free.

What U Mean 2 Me

I saw you off on your R&R one night,
It was then that I knew that something wasn't right.
I knew this day was coming and you had to leave,
But as it became real, I just couldn't believe.

I tried to stay strong and be a man,
But my heart had me questioning whether I can.
My feet got antsy and started to move,
I then realize that I was beginning to lose my grove.

I wanted to walk left, but my feet went right,
It was then I realized it wasn't about my might.
I wanted to stay still and try not to move,
But with my eyes watering, I'll look like a fool.

I wanted to hold you close to my heart,
Knowing that it pains me when we are apart.
I wanted to tell you, in my arms you belong,
But under these rules, some say it would be wrong.

I wanted to tell you that there is love in this place,
But, I felt the shock would send you to an early grave.
You know that I will treat you kind,
But this you will have to accept in your mind.

You knocked me off my feet with the "Kiss",
Now, you have sealed the fact that you will be missed.
When I close my eyes, I still see you,
Then I'll awake and your absence makes me blue.

I'm trying to prepare for you to go away,
But man oh man; how I wish that you would stay.
I was disappointed that I fell asleep on your lap,
But you caressed my head and let me take a nap.

This act alone was very big you see,
Cause it sealed the fact that you have love for me.
Now I know you must hit the road too,
But don't worry; I'll soon be coming just for you.

What's Really Going On?

Hello Baby, I haven't heard from you today,
I checked my phone and no calls came my way.
I guess that you were real busy at work,
But you know when I don't hear from you, I go berserk.

I said that she must be waiting for tonight,
Because that would be the only thing that seem right.
While at work, my thoughts were only of you,
It got so bad that I didn't know what to do.

I went outside to help ease my pain,
Then I noticed that the sky was full of rain.
The rain was pounding all around,
It was so hard that you could hear it hit the ground.

I wanted to run through the rain and get all wet,
Then I thought about the pain and fever that I could get.
I went back in to seek relief,
The thundering and lightening was disbelief.

I began to gather my things as it got close to five,
I didn't know whether to run, walk or even drive.
After the hustle, the traffic, I finally made it in,
I took off my wet clothes and retired to the den.

I checked my voicemail and still no call,
I didn't understand, not one bit at all.
That night I finally got through and you answered the cell,
I had an attitude; I said "what the hell".

You were all polite as you spoke on the phone,
I didn't know how to act; I asked "what's going on"?
I had a busy day and I'm tired you see,
Can you call me later and get back to me?

Get back to you; is that what you said?
Just give me a call before you go to bed.
I said ok, and departed with "I love you",
She didn't reply as usual, but said "me too".

When I Go

When I leave my Earthly home,
I don't want any sadness because I'm gone.
I'm going to a better place,
I've finished my role and endured the race.

I tried to live a good and fruitful life,
There were times when I endured tremendous strife.
I've prepared myself for this day,
Because I knew that this was the only way.

I tried to treat everybody kind,
Even those that pretended to be a friend of mine.
Some of you will miss me more than others,
Some could care less because I ruffled your feathers.

You can't say anything that can change my path,
I've stood the test and I'm ready for the wrath.
I don't know whether I was considered old,
I did all I could, you see that was my goal.

If I offended or shared words of wisdom with you,
Then it was probably for something that you didn't do.
You need to evaluate your life while you still can,
Please remember Christ gave us all a plan.

Some say the good will out weigh the bad,
If you are thinking like that, then you are still sad.
There are still some, who say that this day is far from me,
I'm going to continue to party until I'm around 63.

Keep partying and doing your own thing,
Pretty soon or later, your life phone will ring.
Nobody knows the time or the day,
One thing for sure you will be going this way.

For me, don't cry or fall all over the floor,
Just remember I answered the knock when Christ came to my door.

When We Met

You know me and I know you,
We don't play games as young folks do.
I've known you for quite a long time,
I sometimes get disillusioned and think of you as being mine.

I have to remember you are a single girl,
No one to answer to; just enjoy your own world.
I remember the day when we first met,
I was good as gone, but I held my best.

A fly girl was standing right in front of me,
A sight so pleasing for the eyes to see.
You seemed to be elsewhere and had began to sob,
I didn't think twice and contributed it to the job.

I said it's not that bad, you can tell me,
You said, well it's kind of personal you see.
I offered you a hankie and a helping hand,
Of course I knew it involved some kind of man.

You gave me the short version that applied to you,
I offered my services and said this is what I can do.
You accepted my help and became my friend,
You confided and said; I'll remember you to the end.

Now I'm in a place where loneliness abides,
I appreciate the fact that you stayed by my side.

Why Play Games

If you have something on your mind let it be known,
You aren't a kid anymore, you are full grown.
Sometimes you throw hints and play with words,
But all that stuff went out with the birds.

Speak your mind if you have something to say,
The future is not promised so say it today.
You hold your tongue instead of speaking your mind,
There is no rule to say life has to be kind.

We have known each other for more than a while,
And still you clam up and act like a child.
A grown woman you are as you said to me,
So why when it comes to us, you said you will see?

I'm a man, so don't hold your words back,
You fiddle around and then you retract.
Well, I've said all that I have to say,
When you stop playing games then come my way.

Yes I Do

When I first saw your face,
Your beauty and charm left me amazed.
My heart told me there was something special about you,
And I knew that you were the woman to whom I would say I Do.

Whenever I would leave and have to depart,
It was like I left with only half of my heart.
I'm going to make our life better and new,
It's part of the promise that I made to you.

You are very special in every way,
I think of you and miss you each day.
I'm trying to hang on for as long as I can,
God knows I'm ready to leave this holy land.

Some days things are pretty rough,
It's then that I have to get very tough.
I have to stick it out because you gave me your hand,
It's in the promise to stick to the plan.

That is why on this special day,
I have these words that I want to say.
I want to spend the rest of my life with you,
So before God I declare my love and say "Oh yes I Do".

Yes I Am THICK

I went out on the other day,
It was with a brother that was referred my way.
He called me with a few questions you see,
He wanted to know a few things about me.

I told him I don't normally do the blind date thing,
The last one I had ended in a big scene.
Everything I've heard about you was very tight,
Who knows, this may be your lucky night.

He started by saying he is a man with pride,
He loves to go places with a nice trophy hanging on his side.
Well I am a trophy as I consider myself to be,
My good attitude and smarts is what makes up me.

I'm a fair skinned woman with big brown eyes,
I've got long black hair and some meat on my thighs.
I carry myself with high expectation,
To go along with my college education.

If your ideal of a trophy is tall and thin,
We can cut the chit chat and bring this to an end.
Don't be so quiet unless you are sick,
Yes I am a woman whom is considered thick.

Yesterday

As I sat in my office reflecting about the day,
My mind was on what happened on yesterday.
Sometimes I ignore the facts you see,
Especially when I'm only thinking about me.

I knew that this day would come,
But for years, I ignored it and tried to act dumb.
I bought roses, jewelry and gave you wine,
On occasion we would even go out and dine.

The drugs and booze, I didn't mind,
Because the results was normally a good time.
After a few years and nothing changed,
It began to feel weird and kind of strange.

There were days when you were just pure delight,
Then there were times when you were high as a kite.
I asked did it have to be this way,
You said that you were going to change one day.

I began to distance myself and said my good-byes,
Truly I was hurt as tears fell from my eyes.
I knew I had to go and get away,
Because I would be affected if I chose to stay.

When I went to sleep on that Wednesday night,
I tossed and turned, because something wasn't right.
You see, I got a call late on yesterday,
And the call said simply, your best friend has passed away.

You Are No LADY

You are not a lady as you proclaim to be,
We all know it because we can plainly see.
You speak vulgar words in your talk,
You bounce from side to side in the way you walk.

Your attire is short and extremely tight,
You carry yourself like a woman of the night.
Your fingers snap to your own beat,
And you wonder why a good man is hard to meet.

Some men are looking for what you present,
When they get what they want-then away you will be sent.
You say that men tell you that you are fly,
It's probably what they say when they kiss you goodbye.

A lady has some charm and grace,
You can even see the eloquence upon her face.
She don't jiggle or bounce from side to side,
She has perfected her walk and has rhythm in her glide.

The right man would consider her his queen,
Then he will be glad to serve as her king.

You Came Into My Life.

As I sit in this lonely place,
All I see is the smile upon your face.
I think back to that July day,
Your presence was sent my way.

I find that I'm very sad when we are apart,
Because you have grooved a place in my heart.
Anytime without you seem very long,
Cause it's in my arms that you belong.

I know that I can hang on in,
Cause you are the prize that I long to win.
I can see a great day unfolding,
Especially when it's you – I'll be holding.

I'm going for the gusto as you can see,
Cause I plan on making you my wife to be.
We have the makeup for something grand,
And it's that make up that I'll take my stand.

I'll be so glad when it's that time,
And I'll be able to say that she is all mine.
Everyone shall see what I see,
And that is she really loves me.

I'll take my place and look like a king,
And be proud to present you with that 5 carat ring.
You will have something old, new and blue,
But I'll be waiting for the words "I Do".

The Pastor will turn and say to the crowd,
I have a new introduction to make to you all.
As we stand tall and firm you see,
He will present my new wife and me.

You Will See The Light

I was out way past the midnight hour,
I knew that my wife would be very sour.
I'm the man so I would do it my way,
I won't worry about what she has to say.

It was about three when I quietly opened the door,
Soon there was a voice that said "you are rotten to the core".
Oh, I was out with Billy and the boys,
You know how it is when we are racing our man toys.

I told you about coming in this late,
I'm going to have to show you, I'm the one you must appreciate.
Go ahead and bathe or get your butt in the shower,
When you get finished, we'll discuss my woman power.

I'm pretty tired, can we just go to sleep,
Another hour won't be a problem, I'm sure you will keep.
Did you think about the time when you were doing your thing?
We may have a bigger problem because I don't see your wedding ring.

It's in my pocket; I didn't want to get it wet,
We will discuss it later, this you can bet.
You left around nine going out to roam,
You must have forgotten that you had a home.

We will have this talk only once tonight,
Then there is no doubt you will see the light.

Your Shield Came Down

As we were talking and I complimented you,
You got nervous suddenly right out of the blue.
Something happened if I must say,
I never thought that it would be today.

I don't know what happened but by heart began to race,
All I could see was the beauty of your face.
What did I do to cause this thing?
It's more of a reaction when you get a ring.

Your guard is always up 24 hours a day,
But you must realize that love will come your way.
It may not be in your plans for this,
But clearly it's felt as something you miss.

You put up your guard and take a stand,
I don't know who is going to be the lucky man.
It's natural to fight the way you do,
But love will come and overwhelm you.

I thought that I was a complicated man,
Then I met my equal by the name of Ms. Ann.
She puts up a bold and a terrific fight,
But she will purr like a kitten the first time she spends the night.

Your Smile

I will never forget the smile on your face the first day,
I thought someone had sent an angel my way.
I looked again to be sure of what I had seen,
Then I immediately stared at the finger for a wedding ring.

The wedding ring wasn't there for me to see,
But then it wasn't like I was clear and free.
So I just looked and admired from afar,
If I had my way, I'll be where you are.

A lady you are, short and sweet,
God gave you everything to make you complete.
You say my name with such a beautiful tone,
It sends quivers all the way through my bones.

Seeing you everyday keeps my soul in a blaze,
Sometimes I have to go and put cold water on my face.
It's not everyday that I'll walk a mile,
It's all for the glory of seeing your beautiful smile.

About the Author

The author was born in Houston Texas where he still resides today. He attended HISD secondary schools and graduated from Texas Southern University with a BS degree in Mathematics. After 15 years in management and being on the receiving end of "right-sizing" by several companies, he joined a branch of the government and began a new career. He received recognition for being an outstanding achiever in 1995. In 1998, he received a patent for developing a product "D-Wash net" that kept the dishes from being tossed about in the home dishwasher. One day in 2004, he was told about employment opportunities that existed overseas. After weighing employment options, he boarded a plane in May 2004 and 20 hours later, he found himself exiting the plane in Kuwait. After being in Kuwait for 6 days, he learned that his fate would be truly tested because the decision had been made that his group was heading north into Iraq. He signed for his ballistic helmet and bullet-proofed vest and convoyed to the holy city of Babylon. He soon departed Babylon and headed for a Diwaniyah, south of Baghdad. Diwaniyah is where he began writing. He began to write poems about things that he saw and things that was personal to him as well as things that friends talked about. Now three years later, he has written over 100 poems and has decided to share his story with people of all ages. "Poems from the Sand" is his first book.

Printed in the United States
154117LV00004B/37/A